Grass, Günter
Selected poems

DATE DUE

MAR 13 '74			
NOV 16 '83			
NOV 7 '90			

SELECTED POEMS

GÜNTER GRASS

Selected Poems

IN GERMAN WITH TRANSLATIONS BY
MICHAEL HAMBURGER &
CHRISTOPHER MIDDLETON

HARCOURT, BRACE & WORLD, INC.
NEW YORK

The following translations have appeared before: "Open Wardrobe" "The School for Tenors", "Prevention of Cruelty to Animals" and "Transformation" in *Modern German Poetry 1910-1960*, an Anthology with Verse Translations, edited and with an Introduction by Michael Hamburger and Christopher Middleton, published by Grove Press, Inc., copyright © 1962 by Michael Hamburger & Christopher Middleton; "Unsuccessful Raid" and "Family Matters" in *Evergreen Review*, Volume 9, Number 36, June 1965, copyright © 1965 by Evergreen Review, Inc.; "The Midge Plague", "Open Air Concert" and "Sale" in *The Times Literary Supplement*; "Folding Chairs", "Happiness", "Normandy", "The Sea Battle", "Askesis" and "Chefs and Spoons" in *Encounter*.

Printed in Great Britain by
Fletcher & Son Ltd, Norwich

CONTENTS

The poems on the following pages
were translated by Michael Hamburger:
11, 17, 21, 25, 27, 29,
35, 37, 39, 43, 45, 47,
53, 55, 57

The poems on the following pages
were translated by Christopher Middleton:
9, 13, 15, 23, 31, 49, 51, 61

AN ALLE GÄRTNER

Warum wollt ihr mir verbieten Fleisch zu essen?
Jetzt kommt ihr mit Blumen,
bereitet mir Astern zu,
als bliebe vom Herbst nicht Nachgeschmack genug.
Laßt die Nelken im Garten.
Sind die Mandeln doch bitter,
der Gasometer,
den ihr den Kuchen nennt—
und ihr schneidet mir ab,
bis ich nach Milch verlange.
Ihr sagt: Gemüse,—
und verkauft mir Rosen im Kilo.
Gesund, sagt ihr und meint die Tulpen.
Soll ich das Gift,
zu kleinen Sträußchen gebunden,
mit etwas Salz verspeisen?
Soll ich an Maiglöckchen sterben?
Und die Lilien auf meinem Grab,—
wer wird mich vor den Vegetariern schützen?

Laßt mich vom Fleisch essen.
Laßt mich mit dem Knochen alleine,
damit er die Scham verliert und sich nackt zeigt
Erst wenn ich vom Teller rücke
und den Ochsen laut ehre,
dann erst öffnet die Gärten,
damit ich Blumen kaufen kann—
weil ich sie gerne welken sehe.

TO ALL GARDENERS

Why should you tell me to eat no meat?
Now you come to me with flowers,
prepare asters,
as if autumn's aftertaste was not enough.
Leave the carnations in the garden.
So what, the almonds are bitter,
the gasometer
which you call the cake—
and you cut me a piece
till I ask for milk.
You say: vegetables—
and sell me roses by the kilo.
Healthy, you say, and mean the tulips.
Should I eat with some salt
the poison
tied in little bunches?
Should I die of lilies-of-the-valley?
And the lilies on my grave—
who'll protect me from the vegetarians?

Let me eat meat.
Let me be, with the bone.
Let the bone lose all shame and show itself naked.
Only when I rise from the plate
and loudly do the ox honour,
only then open up the gardens
for me to buy flowers—
because I like to see them dying.

GEÖFFNETER SCHRANK

Unten stehen die Schuhe.
Sie fürchten sich vor einem Käfer
auf dem Hinweg,
vor einem Pfennig auf dem Rückweg,
vor Käfer und Pfennig die sie treten könnten
bis es sich einprägt.
Oben ist die Heimat der Hüte.
Behüte, hüte dich, behutsam.
Unglaubliche Federn,
wie hieß der Vogel,
wohin rollte sein Blick
als er einsah, daß er zu bunt geraten?
Die weißen Kugeln, die in den Taschen schlafen,
träumen von Motten.
Hier fehlt ein Knopf,
im Gürtel ermüdet die Schlange.
Schmerzliche Seide,
Astern und andere feuergefährliche Blumen,
der Herbst, der zum Kleid wird,
jeden Sonntag mit Fleisch und dem Salz
gefälteter Wäsche gefüllt.
Bevor der Schrank schweigt, Holz wird,
ein entfernter Verwandter der Kiefer,—
wer wird den Mantel tragen
wenn du einmal tot bist?
Seinen Arm im Ärmel bewegen,
zuvorkommend jeder Bewegung?
Wer wird den Kragen hochschlagen,
vor den Bildern stehen bleiben
und alleine sein unter der windigen Glocke?

OPEN WARDROBE

The shoes are at the bottom.
They are afraid of a beetle
on the way out,
of a penny on the way back,
of a beetle and a penny on which they might tread
till it impresses itself.
At the top is the home of the headgear.
Take heed, be wary, not headstrong.
Incredible feathers,
what was the bird called,
where did its eyes roll
when it knew that its wings were too gaudy?
The white balls asleep in the pockets
dream of moths.
Here a button is missing,
in this belt the snake grows weary.
Doleful silk,
asters and other inflammable flowers,
autumn becoming a dress.
Every Sunday filled with flesh
and the salt of creased linen.
Before the wardrobe falls silent, turns into wood,
a distant relation of pine-trees—
who will wear the coat
one day when you're dead?
Who move his arm in the sleeve,
anticipate every movement?
Who will turn up the collar,
stop in front of the pictures
and be alone under the windy cloche?

HOCHWASSER

Wir warten den Regen ab,
obgleich wir uns daran gewöhnt haben
hinter der Gardine zu stehen, unsichtbar zu sein.
Löffel ist Sieb geworden, niemand wagt mehr
die Hand auszustrecken.
Es schwimmt jetzt Vieles in den Straßen
das man während der trockenen Zeit sorgfältig verbarg.
Wie peinlich des Nachbarn verbrauchte Betten zu sehen.
Oft stehen wir vor dem Pegel
und vergleichen unsere Besorgnis wie Uhren.
Manches läßt sich regulieren.
Doch wenn die Behälter überlaufen, das ererbte Maß voll ist,
werden wir beten müssen.
Der Keller steht unter Wasser, wir haben die Kisten hochgetragen
und prüfen den Inhalt mit der Liste.
Noch ist nichts verloren gegangen.—
Weil das Wasser jetzt sicher bald fällt
haben wir begonnen Sonnenschirmchen zu nähen.
Es wird sehr schwer sein wieder über den Platz zu gehen,
deutlich, mit bleischwerem Schatten.
Wir werden den Vorhang am Anfang vermissen
und oft in den Keller steigen
um den Strich zu betrachten,
den das Wasser uns hinterließ.

THE FLOOD

We are waiting for the rain to stop,
although we have got accustomed
to standing behind the curtain, being invisible.
Spoons have become sieves, nobody dares now
to stretch a hand out.
Many things are floating in the streets,
things people carefully hid in the dry time.
How awkward to see your neighbour's stale old beds.
Often we stand by the water-gauge
and compare our worries like watches.
Some things can be regulated.
But when the butts overflow, the inherited cup fills,
we shall have to pray.
The cellar is submerged, we brought the crates up
and are checking their contents against the list.
So far nothing has been lost.
Because the water is now certain to drop soon,
we have begun to sew sunshades.
It will be difficult to cross the square once more,
distinct, with a shadow heavy as lead.
We shall miss the curtain at first,
and go into the cellar often
to consider the mark
which the water bequeathed us.

DIE MÜCKENPLAGE

In unserem Bezirk wird es von Jahr zu Jahr schlimmer.
Oft laden wir Besuch um den Schwarm etwas zu teilen.
Doch die Leute gehen bald wieder,—
nachdem sie den Käse gelobt haben.

Es ist nicht der Stich.
Nein, das Gefühl, daß etwas geschieht,
das älter ist als die Hand—
und im Besitz jeder Zukunft.

Wenn die Betten still sind
und der schwarze Stein an unzähligen, tönenden Fäden hängt,
Fäden die reißen und wieder neu,
etwas heller beginnen,

wenn ich eine Pfeife anbrenne
und nach dem See hin sitze,
auf dem ein dichtes Geräusch schwimmt,
bin ich hilflos.

Wir wollen jetzt nicht mehr schlafen.
Meine Söhne sind hellwach,
die Töchter drängen vor dem Spiegel,
meine Frau hat Kerzen gestellt.

Nun glauben wir an Flammen,
die zwanzig Pfennige kosten,
denen die Mücken sich nähern,
einer kurzen Verheißung.

THE MIDGE PLAGUE

It's getting worse hereabouts every year.
Often we have guests in, to share the swarm.
But soon people leave again—
having commended the cheese.

It's not the sting.
No, but the sense that what's going on
is older than the hand—
and has every future in its grasp.

When the beds go quiet
and the black stone hangs by innumerable singing threads,
threads which break and start again,
mended, a little more clear,

when I light a pipe
and sit facing the lake
with a thick sound swimming over it,
I'm helpless.

Let's give up trying to sleep.
My sons are wide awake,
my daughters crowd to the mirror,
my wife has lit candles.

Now we pin our faith on flames
costing twenty pfennigs,
which the midges come to,
a brief promise.

DIE SCHULE DER TENÖRE

Nimm den Lappen, wische den Mond fort,
schreibe die Sonne, die andere Münze
über den Himmel, die Schultafel.
Setze dich dann.
Dein Zeugnis wird gut sein,
du wirst versetzt werden,
eine neue, hellere Mütze tragen.
Denn die Kreide hat recht
und der Tenor der sie singt.
Er wird den Samt entblättern,
Efeu, Meterware der Nacht,
Moos, ihren Unterton,
jede Amsel wird er vertreiben.

Den Bassisten, mauert ihn ein
in seinem Gewölbe.
Wer glaubt noch an Fässer
in denen der Wein fällt?
Ob Vogel oder Schrapnell,
oder nur Summen bis es knackt,
weil der Äther überfüllt ist
mit Wochenend und Sommerfrische.
Scheren, die in den Schneiderstuben
das Lied von Frühling und Konfektion zwitschern,—
hieran kein Beispiel.

Die Brust heraus, bis der Wind seinen Umweg macht.
Immer wieder Trompeten,
spitzgedrehte Tüten voller silberner Zwiebeln.
Dann die Geduld.
Warten, bis der Dame die Augen davonlaufen,
zwei unzufriedene Dienstmädchen.

THE SCHOOL FOR TENORS

Take your duster, wipe away the moon,
write the sun, that other coin
across the sky, the blackboard.
Then take your seat.
Your report will be a good one,
You will go up one class,
wear a new, a brighter cap.
For the chalk is in the right
and so is the tenor who sings it.
He will unroll the velvet,
ivy, yard-measured wares of night,
moss, its undertone,
every blackbird he'll drive away.

The bass—immure him
in his vault.
Who now believes in barrels
in which the wine-level falls?
Whether bird or shrapnel
or only a hum till it cracks
because the ether is overcrowded
with weekend and sea-side resort.
Scissors which in the tailors' workshops
twitter the song of springtime and haute couture—
this no example.

Puff out your chest, till the wind takes its devious way.
Trumpets again and again,
conical paper bags full of silver onions.
After that, patience.
Wait till the lady's eyes run away,
two dissatisfied skivvies.

Jetzt erst den Ton den die Gläser fürchten
und der Staub
der die Gesimse verfolgt bis sie hinken.

Fischgräten, wer singt diese Zwischenräume,
den Mittag, mit Schilf gespießt?
Wie schön sang Else Fenske, als sie,
während der Sommerferien,
in großer Höhe daneben trat,
in einen stillen Gletscherspalt stürzte,
uns nur ihr Schirmchen
und das hohe C zurückließ.

Das hohe C, die vielen Nebenflüsse des Mississippi,
der herrliche Atem,
der die Kuppeln erfand und den Beifall.
Vorhang, Vorhang, Vorhang.
Schnell, bevor der Leuchter nicht mehr klirren will,
bevor die Galerien knicken
und die Seide billig wird.
Vorhang, bevor du den Beifall begreifst.

Only now that tone which the glasses fear
and the dust
that pursues the ledges until they limp.

Fishbones, who will sing these gaps,
sing noon impaled with rushes?
How well did Elsie Fenner sing
when, in the summer vacation
at a great height she took a false step,
tumbled into a silent glacier crevasse
and left nothing behind but
her little parasol and the high C.

The high C, the many tributaries of the Mississippi,
the glorious breath
that invented cupolas and applause.
Curtain, curtain, curtain.
Quick before the candelabrum refuses to jingle,
before the galleries droop
and silk becomes cheap.
Curtain, before you understand the applause.

MUSIK IM FREIEN

Als die Pause überwunden schien,
kam Aurele mit dem Knochen.
Seht meine Flöte und mein weißes Hemd,
seht die Giraffe die über den Zaun späht,
das ist mein Blut, welches zuhört.
Nun will ich alle Drosseln besiegen.

Als der gelbe Hund über die Wiese lief
verendete das Konzert.
Später fand man den Knochen nicht mehr.
Die Noten lagen unter den Stühlen,
der Kapellmeister nahm sein Luftgewehr
und erschoß alle Amseln.

OPEN AIR CONCERT

When the interval seemed to have been overcome
Aurelia arrived with the bone.
Look at my flute and my white shift,
look at the giraffe peering over the fence,
those are my blood, which is listening.
Now I'll defeat all the thrushes.

When the yellow dog ran over the meadow
the concert expired.
Later the bone could not be found.
The scores lay under the chairs,
the conductor seized his air-gun
and shot all the blackbirds.

DIE KLINGEL

Versuche mit Tinte,
Niederschriften im Rauch,
halb erwacht
im Dickicht süßer Gardinen.
Die Straße, den Notverband wieder aufgerollt
weil die Wunde juckt,
weil die Erinnerung sich stückeln läßt und längen
so eine Katze unterm Streicheln.

Wer bewegte die Klingel,
belud die Luft mit Erfolg.
War es das Glück,
mit neuen, dünneren Strümpfen
oder der Mann
mit dem Krankenschein unter der Haut.
Niemand erschrak. Nicht das Wasser zum Spülen,
kleinen Frauen im Zimmer kräuselte sauer der Rock.

Wer kann eine Klingel wieder verkaufen,
zurücktreten, mit dem Hut in der Hand,
die Kreide der Herkunft vom Zaun lecken.
Die nackte Gestalt wird zwischen den Spiegeln
keinen Vorsprung gewinnen.
Keine Bewegung kommt hier zu kurz.
Gleichzeitig wird es hüsteln,
das Weiße im Auge vergilben,
der falsche Bart,
ein letztes Geständnis,
von der Oberlippe wird sich der Rauch lösen
und keinen Vogel begeistern.

THE DOORBELL

Essays with ink,
inscribings in the smoke,
half wakened
in the thicket of sweet curtains.
The street, the bandage rolled up again,
because the wound is twitching,
because memory can be assembled and stretched—
some cat being stroked.

Who pushed the bell,
loaded the air with success.
Was it happiness
with new, sheerer stockings,
or the man
with the medical card under his skin.
No one jumped. Not the dish water,
sourly the skirts of little women crinkled in the room.

Who can sell back a doorbell,
withdraw, hat in hand,
lick from the fence his origin's chalk-mark.
The naked figure will not get ahead
between the mirrors.
Here no motion falls too short.
There'll be a slight simultaneous coughing,
the whites of eyes yellowing,
the false beard,
a last admission,
smoke shall be loosed from the upper lip
and excite no bird.

DER ELFTE FINGER

Wo blieb mein elfter Finger,
mein elfter, besonderer Finger,
niemals hat er gelacht,
niemals den Handschuh, die Nacht
wegen der Farbe getragen.
Er hat die Ziege gemelkt.
Er hat die Ziege gemelkt,
hat die Ziege der Uhr zugetrieben,
die Ziege hat sich gebückt.
Konnte sich bücken, konnte der Uhr,
hat der Uhr die Sohlen geleckt,
bis die Uhr kicherte, kicherte,
alle Minuten verlor,
alles, auch ihre Pausen gestand.
Nun sah er im Weiten schon Gold,
der Finger sah weither schon Gold,
hat Juweliere verführt,
Bräute, kurz vor der Kirche.
Schlüssel war er, Stempel, Verschweigen,—
oft habe ich meinen elften Finger geschleckt,,
obgleich er niemals schlief,
obgleich er niemals schlief.

Worauf soll ich nun deuten?
Worauf soll ich nun deuten,
heute, da beide verkürzten Hände
nur noch geschickt sind
Eisen wie Fleisch, Fleisch, einen Amboß zu tasten,—
oder sie hocken am Abend gleich belasteten Krähen
auf einem Stein im Feld,
zählen acht, neun, zehn, niemals elf.
Niemals zählen sie elf.

THE ELEVENTH FINGER

Where is my eleventh finger,
my eleventh, my special finger,
not once has it laughed,
not once worn the glove, the night
because of their colour.
It milked the goat.
It milked the goat,
and drove the goat to the clock;
the goat bent down.
Was able to bend, could lick,
did lick the soles of the clock
till the clock tittering, tittering,
lost all its minutes, made
a clean breast of everything, even the stops.
Now far off it saw gold,
the finger saw gold from afar,
a seducer of jewellers, brides
on the very threshold of churches.
A key it was, a stamp, a silence—
often I've sucked my eleventh finger
although it never slept,
although it never slept.

At what am I now to point?
At what am I now to point,
today, when both my shortened hands
are good for nothing but
to feel flesh like iron, flesh, and an anvil—
or evenings they crouch like dejected crows
on a stone in a field,
counting eight, nine, ten, never eleven—
they never count eleven.

TIERSCHUTZ

Das Klavier in den Zoo.
Schnell, bringt das Zebra in die gute Stube.
Seid freundlich mit ihm,
es kommt aus Bechstein.
Noten frißt es
und unsere süßen Ohren.

NÄCHTLICHES STADION

Langsam ging der Fußball am Himmel auf.
Nun sah man, daß die Tribüne besetzt war.
Einsam stand der Dichter im Tor,
doch der Schiedsrichter pfiff: Abseits.

MISSLUNGENER ÜBERFALL

Am Mittwoch.
Jeder wußte wieviele Treppen hinauf,
den Druck auf den Knopf,
die zweite Tür links.
Sie stürmten die Kasse.
Es war aber Sonntag
und das Geld in der Kirche.

FAMILIÄR

In unserem Museum,—wir besuchen es jeden Sonntag,—
hat man eine neue Abteilung eröffnet.
Unsere abgetriebenen Kinder, blasse, ernsthafte Embryos,
sitzen dort in schlichten Gläsern
und sorgen sich um die Zukunft ihrer Eltern.

PREVENTION OF CRUELTY TO ANIMALS

The piano into the zoo.
Quick, get the zebra into the best room.
Be kind to it,
it comes from Bechstein.
Scores are its fodder,
and our sweet ears.

STADIUM AT NIGHT

Slowly the football rose in the sky.
Now one could see that the stands were packed.
Alone the poet stood at the goal
but the referee whistled: Off-side.

UNSUCCESSFUL RAID

On Wednesday.
Everyone knew how many steps,
which bell to ring,
the second door on the left.
They smashed the till.
But it was Sunday
and the cash was at church.

FAMILY MATTERS

In our museum—we always go there on Sundays—
they have opened a new department.
Our aborted children, pale, serious embryos,
sit there in plain glass jars
and worry about their parents' future.

MÖBEL IM FREIEN

Wer warf die Gartenbank um?
Nun liegt sie da, grün und vergeblich,
stottert mit vier bewiesenen Beinen,
sucht den Beweis in der Luft.
Aufstellen wieder. Wieder wie vorher
unter dem Sommer sitzen und Kaffee
mit einer Tante trinken und Kekse,
Hostien brechen.

Nein, dieser Sommer ist pleite.
Die Tante nährt weiße Würmer,
die Kekse krümeln und passen
in keine ererbte Monstranz.
Auch trinkst du den Kaffee
zu heiß, halb im Weggehn,
flüchtig, mit sichernden Blicken
nach links, nach rechts und nach links.

Gartenbänke die einmal gestürzt,
stehen nun ledig, kundig des Herbstes,
zwischen den nassen Stachelbeersträuchern,
vom Regen, Aufbruch, mitten im Satz,
vom Mond der nie stillsitzt bevölkert.

FURNITURE OUT OF DOORS

Who up-ended the garden seat?
Now here it lies, useless and green,
stammers with four proven legs,
looks for the proof in the air.
Stand it up again. As before
to sit beneath the summer,
drink tea with an aunt and break
biscuits, holy wafers.

No, this summer is done for.
The aunt is feeding white worms,
the biscuits are crumbling and fit
into no inherited pyx.
Also, you're drinking your tea
too hot, on the point of leaving,
rushed, with defensive glances
to the left, to the right, to the left.

Once up-ended, garden seats
stand vacant, conscious of autumn,
between wet gooseberry bushes,
occupied only by rain, departure, the sentence cut short,
by the moon that never sits still.

BLECHMUSIK

Damals schliefen wir in einer Trompete.
Es war sehr still dort,
wir träumten von keinem Signal,
lagen, wie zum Beweis,
mit offenem Mund in der Schlucht,—
damals, ehe wir ausgestoßen.

War es ein Kind, auf dem Kopf
einen Helm aus gelesener Zeitung,
war es ein irrer Husar
der auf Befehl aus dem Bild trat,
war es schon damals der Tod,
der so seinen Stempel behauchte?

Heute, ich weiß nicht wer uns geweckt hat,
vermummt als Blumen in Vasen
oder in Zuckerdosen,
von jedem bedroht der Kaffee trinkt
und sein Gewissen befragt:
Ein oder zwei Stückchen oder gar drei.

Nun fliehen wir und mit uns unser Gepäck.
Alle halbleeren Tüten, jeden Trichter im Bier,
kaum verlassene Mäntel, stehengebliebene Uhren,
Gräber die andre bezahlten
und Frauen die sehr wenig Zeit haben,
füllen wir kurzfristig aus.

In Schubladen voller Wäsche und Liebe,
in einem Ofen der Nein sagt
und nur seinen Standpunkt erwärmt,
in einem Telefon blieben unsere Ohren zurück
und hören, nun schon versöhnlich,
dem neuen Zeichen Besetzt zu.

MUSIC FOR BRASS

Those days we slept in a trumpet.
It was very quiet in there,
we never dreamed it would sound,
lay, as if to prove it,
open-mouthed in the gorge—
those days, before we were blown out.

Was it a child, on his head
a helmet of studied newspaper,
was it a scatty hussar
who walked at a command out of the picture,
was it even those days death
who breathed that way on his rubber stamp?

Today, I don't know who woke us,
disguised as flowers in vases,
or else in sugar bowls,
threatened by anyone who drinks coffee
and questions his conscience:
one lump or two, or even three.

Now we're on the run and our luggage with us.
All half-empty paper bags, every crater in our beer,
cast-off coats, clocks that have stopped,
graves paid for by other people,
and women very short of time,
for a while we fill them.

In drawers full of linen and love,
in a stove which says no
and warms its own standpoint only,
in a telephone our ears have stayed behind
and listen, already conciliant,
to the new tone for busy.

Damals schliefen wir in einer Trompete.
Hin und zurück träumten wir,
Alleen gleichmäßig bepflanzt.
Auf ruhigem, endlosem Rücken
lagen wir jenem Gewölbe an
und träumten von keinem Signal.

Those days we slept in a trumpet.
Backward and forward we dreamed,
avenues, symmetrically planted.
On a tranquil unending back
we lay against that arch,
and never dreamed it would sound.

WANDLUNG

Plötzlich waren die Kirschen da,
obgleich ich vergessen hatte,
daß es Kirschen gibt
und verkünden ließ: Noch nie gab es Kirschen—
waren sie da, plötzlich und teuer.

Pflaumen fielen und trafen mich.
Doch wer da denkt,
ich wandelte mich,
weil etwas fiel und mich traf,
wurde noch nie von fallenden Pflaumen getroffen.

Erst als man Nüsse in meine Schuhe schüttete
und ich laufen mußte,
weil die Kinder die Kerne wollten,
schrie ich nach Kirschen, wollt ich von Pflaumen
getroffen werden—und wandelte mich ein wenig.

TRANSFORMATION

Suddenly the cherries were there
although I had forgotten
that cherries exist
and caused to be proclaimed: There never have been cherries—
they were there, suddenly and dear.

Plums fell and hit me;
but whoever thinks
that I was transformed
because something fell and hit me
has never been hit by falling plums.

Only when they poured nuts into my shoes
and I had to walk
because the children wanted the kernels
I cried out for cherries, wanted plums
to hit me—and was transformed a little.

KLAPPSTÜHLE

Wie traurig sind diese Veränderungen.
Die Leute schrauben ihre Namenschilder ab,
nehmen den Topf mit dem Rotkohl,
wärmen ihn auf, anderen Ortes.

Was sind das für Möbel,
die für den Aufbruch werben?
Die Leute nehmen ihre Klappstühle
und wandern aus.

Mit Heimweh und Brechreiz beladene Schiffe
tragen patentierte Sitzgelegenheiten
und patentlose Besitzer
hin und her.

Auf beiden Seiten des großen Wassers
stehen nun Klappstühle;
wie traurig sind diese Veränderungen.

FOLDING CHAIRS

How sad these changes are.
People unscrew the nameplates from the doors,
take the saucepan of cabbage
and heat it up again, in a different place.

What sort of furniture is this
that advertises departure?
People take up their folding chairs
and emigrate.

Ships laden with homesickness and the urge to vomit
carry patented seating contraptions
and their unpatented owners
to and fro.

Now on both sides of the great ocean
there are folding chairs;
how sad these changes are.

KIRSCHEN

Wenn die Liebe auf Stelzen
über die Kieswege stochert
und in die Bäume reicht,
möchte auch ich gerne Kirschen
in Kirschen als Kirschen erkennen,

nicht mehr mit Armen zu kurz,
mit Leitern, denen es immer
an einer Sprosse mangelt,
von Fallobst leben, Kompott.

Süß und süßer, fast schwarz;
Amseln träumen so rot—
wer küßt hier wen,
wenn die Liebe
auf Stelzen in Bäume reicht.

CHERRIES

When love on stilts
picks its way along gravel paths
and reaches the treetops
I too in cherries would like
to experience cherries as cherries,

no longer with arms too short,
with ladders on which for ever
one rung, just one rung is missing,
to live on stewed fruit, on windfalls.

Sweet and sweeter, darkening;
a red such as blackbirds dream—
who here is kissing whom,
when love
reaches the treetops on stilts.

STAPELLAUF

Wenn es die Möwe verlangt,
werde ich ein Schiff bauen,
werde beim Stapellauf
glücklich sein,
ein blendendes Hemd tragen,
vielleicht auch Sekt weinen
oder Schmierseife absondern,
ohne die es nicht geht.

Wer wird die Rede halten?
Wer kann vom Blatt lesen
ohne zu erblinden?
Der Präsident?
Auf welchen Namen soll ich dich taufen?
Soll ich deinen Untergang ANNA nennen
oder COLUMBUS?

LAUNCHING

If the seagull insists
I shall build a ship,
shall be happy at
the launching,
wear a dazzling shirt,
perhaps also weep champagne
or secrete soft soap,
both being indispensable.

Who will make the speech?
Who can sight-read the words
without going blind?
The President?
By what name shall I christen you?
Shall I call your sinking ANNA
or else COLUMBUS?

IM EI

Wir leben im Ei.
Die Innenseite der Schale
haben wir mit unanständigen Zeichnungen
und den Vornamen unserer Feinde bekritzelt.
Wir werden gebrütet.

Wer uns auch brütet,
unseren Bleistift brütet er mit.
Ausgeschlüpft eines Tages,
werden wir uns sofort
ein Bildnis des Brütenden machen.

Wir nehmen an, daß wir gebrütet werden.
Wir stellen uns ein gutmütiges Geflügel vor
und schreiben Schulaufsätze
über Farbe und Rasse
der uns brütenden Henne.

Wann schlüpfen wir aus?
Unsere Propheten im Ei
streiten sich für mittelmäßige Bezahlung
über die Dauer der Brutzeit.
Sie nehmen einen Tag X an.

Aus Langeweile und echtem Bedürfnis
haben wir Brutkästen erfunden.
Wir sorgen uns sehr um unseren Nachwuchs im Ei.
Gerne würden wir jener, die über uns wacht
unser Patent empfehlen.

Wir aber haben ein Dach überm Kopf.
Senile Küken,
Embryos mit Sprachkenntnissen
reden den ganzen Tag
und besprechen noch ihre Träume.

IN THE EGG

We live in the egg.
We have covered the inside wall
of the shell with dirty drawings
and the Christian names of our enemies.
We are being hatched.

Whoever is hatching us
is hatching our pencils as well.
Set free from the egg one day
at once we shall draw a picture
of whoever is hatching us.

We assume that we're being hatched.
We imagine some good-natured fowl
and write school essays
about the colour and breed
of the hen that is hatching us.

When shall we break the shell?
Our prophets inside the egg
for a middling salary argue
about the period of incubation.
They posit a day called X.

Out of boredom and genuine need
we have invented incubators.
We are much concerned about our offspring inside the egg.
We should be glad to recommend our patent
to her who looks after us.

But we have a roof over our heads.
Senile chicks,
polyglot embryos
chatter all day
and even discuss their dreams.

Und wenn wir nun nicht gebrütet werden?
Wenn diese Schale niemals ein Loch bekommt?
Wenn unser Horizont nur der Horizont
unserer Kritzeleien ist und auch bleiben wird?
Wir hoffen, daß wir gebrütet werden.

Wenn wir auch nur noch vom Brüten reden,
bleibt doch zu befürchten, daß jemand,
außerhalb unserer Schale, Hunger verspürt,
uns in die Pfanne haut und mit Salz bestreut.—
Was machen wir dann, ihr Brüder im Ei?

And what if we're not being hatched?
If this shell will never break?
If our horizon is only that
of our scribbles, and always will be?
We hope that we're being hatched.

Even if we only talk of hatching
there remains the fear that someone
outside our shell will feel hungry
and crack us into the frying pan with a pinch of salt.
What shall we do then, my brethren inside the egg?

GLÜCK

Ein leerer Autobus
stürzt durch die ausgesternte Nacht.
Vielleicht singt sein Chauffeur
und ist glücklich dabei.

NORMANDIE

Die Bunker am Strand
können ihren Beton nicht loswerden.
Manchmal kommt ein halbtoter General
und streichelt Schießscharten.
Oder es wohnen Touristen
für fünf verquälte Minuten—
Wind, Sand, Papier und Urin:
Immer ist Invasion.

DIE SEESCHLACHT

Ein amerikanischer Flugzeugträger
und eine gotische Kathedrale
versenkten sich
mitten im Stillen Ozean
gegenseitig.
Bis zum Schluß
spielte der junge Vikar auf der Orgel.—
Nun hängen Flugzeuge und Engel in der Luft
und können nicht landen.

HAPPINESS

An empty bus
hurtles through the starry night.
Perhaps the driver is singing
and is happy because he sings.

NORMANDY

The pillboxes on the beach
cannot get rid of their concrete.
At times a moribund general
arrives and strokes the loopholes.
Or tourists come to spend
five agonized minutes—
wind, sand, paper and urine:
the invasion goes on.

THE SEA BATTLE

An American aircraft carrier
and a Gothic cathedral
simultaneously sank each other
in the middle of the Pacific.
To the last
the young curate played on the organ.
Now aeroplanes and angels hang in the air
and have nowhere to land.

ASKESE

Die Katze spricht.
Was spricht die Katze denn?
Du sollst mit einem spitzen Blei
die Bräute und den Schnee schattieren,
du sollst die graue Farbe lieben,
unter bewölktem Himmel sein.

Die Katze spricht.
Was spricht die Katze denn?
Du sollst dich mit dem Abendblatt,
in Sacktuch wie Kartoffeln kleiden,
und diesen Anzug immer wieder wenden
und nie in neuem Anzug sein.

Die Katze spricht.
Was spricht die Katze denn?
Du solltest die Marine streichen,
die Kirschen, Mohn und Nasenbluten,
auch jene Fahne sollst du streichen
und Asche auf Geranien streun.

Du sollst, so spricht die Katze weiter,
nur noch von Nieren, Milz und Leber,
von atemloser saurer Lunge,
vom Seich der Nieren, ungewässert,
von alter Milz und zäher Leber,
aus grauem Topf: so sollst du leben.

Und an die Wand, wo früher pausenlos
das grüne Bild das Grüne wiederkäute,
sollst du mit deinem spitzen Blei
Askese schreiben, schreib: Askese.
So spricht die Katze: Schreib Askese.

ASKESIS

The cat speaks.
And what does the cat say?
Thou shalt draw with sharpened pencil
brides of shade and shade of snow,
thou shalt love the colour grey
and be beneath a cloudy sky.

The cat speaks.
And what does the cat say?
Thou shalt be clad in the evening paper,
clad in sackcloth like potatoes,
and thou shalt turn this suit year out year in,
and in a new suit never be.

The cat speaks.
And what does the cat say?
Thou shouldst scratch the navy out;
cherries, poppy, bloody nose
thou shalt scratch out, that flag as well,
and daub geraniums with ash.

Thou, the cat goes on to say,
Shalt live on kidneys, spleen and liver,
lung that's out of breath and sour,
on urine of unsoaked kidneys,
old spleen and tough liver
out of a grey pot: live on that.

And on the wall, where earlier without pause
the ruminant green picture chewed its green,
thou shalt write with thy sharp pencil
this: Askesis; write Askesis.
That's what the cat says: write Askesis.

DIANA—ODER DIE GEGENSTÄNDE

Wenn sie mit rechter Hand
über die rechte Schulter in ihren Köcher greift,
stellt sie das linke Bein vor.

Als sie mich traf,
traf ihr Gegenstand meine Seele,
die ihr wie ein Gegenstand ist.

Zumeist sind es ruhende Gegenstände,
an denen sich montags
mein Knie aufschlägt.

Sie aber, mit ihrem Jagdschein,
läßt sich nur laufend
und zwischen Hunden fotografieren.

Wenn sie ja sagt und trifft,
trifft sie die Gegenstände der Natur
aber auch ausgestopfte.

Immer lehnte ich ab,
von einer schattenlosen Idee
meinen schattenwerfenden Körper verletzen zu lassen.

Doch du, Diana,
mit deinem Bogen
bist mir gegenständlich und haftbar.

DIANA—OR THE OBJECTS

When with her right hand she reaches
over her right shoulder into the quiver,
she puts forward her left leg.

When she hit me,
her object hit my soul
which is to her like an object.

Mostly it is objects resting
against which on Mondays
my knee smashes.

But she, with her hunting permit,
may be photographed only
running and among hounds.

When she says yes and hits,
she hits the objects in nature,
but also stuffed ones.

I have always refused
to let my shadow-casting body
be hurt by a shadowless idea.

But you, Diana,
with your bow,
are to me objective and answerable.

AUSVERKAUF

Ich habe alles verkauft.
Die Leute stiegen vier Treppen hoch,
klingelten zweimal, atemlos
und zahlten mir auf den Fußboden,
weil der Tisch schon verkauft war.

Während ich alles verkaufte,
enteigneten sie fünf oder sechs Straßen weiter
die besitzanzeigenden Fürwörter
und sägten den kleinen harmlosen Männern
den Schatten ab, den privaten.

Ich habe alles verkauft.
Bei mir ist nichts mehr zu holen.
Selbst meinen letzten winzigsten Genitiv,
den ich von früher her anhänglich aufbewahrte,
habe ich günstig verkaufen können.

Alles habe ich verkauft.
Den Stühlen machte ich Beine,
dem Schrank sprach ich das Recht ab,
die Betten stellte ich bloß—
ich legte mich wunschlos daneben.

Am Ende war alles verkauft.
Die Hemden kragen-und hoffnungslos,
die Hosen wußten zuviel,
einem rohen blutjungen Kotelett
schenkte ich meine Bratpfanne

und gleichfalls mein restliches Salz.

SALE

I've sold out, all I owned, the lot.
Four flights of stairs they came up,
rang the bell twice, out of breath,
and paid down their cash on the floor,
since the table too had been sold.

While I was selling it all,
five or six streets from here they expropriated
all the possessive pronouns
and sawed off the private shadows
of little innocuous men.

I've sold out, all I owned, the lot.
There's no more to be had from me.
Even my last and tiniest genitive,
a keepsake long treasured devoutly,
fetched a good price in the end.

All I owned is sold now, the lot.
My old chairs—I sent them packing.
The wardrobe—I gave it the sack.
The beds—I stripped them, exposed them
and lay down beside them, abstemious.

In the end all I'd owned had been sold.
The shirts were collarless, hopeless,
the trousers by now knew too much;
to a raw and blushing young cutlet
I made a gift of my frying-pan

and all that was left of my salt.

KLEINE AUFFORDERUNG ZUM GROSSEN MUNDAUFMACHEN—ODER DER WASSERSPEIER SPRICHT

Wer jene Fäulnis,
die lange hinter der Zahnpaste lebte,
freigeben, ausatmen will,
muß seinen Mund aufmachen.

Wir wollen nun den Mund aufmachen,
die schlimmen Goldzähne,
die wir den Toten brachen und pflückten,
auf Ämtern abliefern.

Um dicke Väter
—jetzt, da auch wir schon Väter und immer dicker—
absetzen und ausspeien zu können,
muß man den Mund aufmachen;

wie unsere Kinder bei Zeiten
den Mund aufmachen, die große Fäulnis,
die schlimmen Goldzähne, die dicken Väter
ausspeien werden, absetzen werden.

LITTLE ADDRESS CALLING FOR A GREAT OPENING OF MOUTHS—OR THE GARGOYLE SPEAKS

Whoever wishes
to release, to breathe out
that caries which long has lurked behind the toothpaste
has no choice but to open his mouth.

Now let us open our mouths,
go to offices and hand in
the bad gold teeth
which we broke and plucked from the dead.

Before you can hope to
displace, to spew out fat fathers—
now that we too are fathers and putting on fat—
you've no choice but to open your mouths;

just as our children in time will
open their mouths, will displace,
will spew out the great caries,
the bad gold teeth, the fat fathers.

KÖCHE UND LÖFFEL

Und manche sagen: Koch ist Koch.
Neu, frischgewaschen und gestärkt,
im Schneefall und vor heller Wand
bleiben die Köche unbemerkt,
und nur der Löffel in der Hand
rührt uns, läßt niemanden vergessen:
Die Köche geben uns zu essen.

Wir sollten nicht von Suppen sprechen
—der Suppenkohl kann nicht dafür—
denn Hunger heißt nur, Vorwand für ein Bier,
und Überdruß leckt jedem Löffel Flächen
und sitzt und zählt die Schritte bis zur Tür.

Die Puppen überleben sich,
der Hahn stirbt vor dem Koch
und kräht woanders, dennoch zittern
in dieser Stadt manchmal die Scheiben.
Die Puppen überleben sich,
der Hahn stirbt vor dem Koch.

Es liegt am Fleisch, der Koch lebt nur im Geist.
Die Zeit vergeht, das Rindfleisch wird nicht weich,
wird später, wird im Schlaf noch dauern,
wird zwischen deinen Zähnen kauern;
es liegt am Fleisch, der Koch lebt nur im Geist.

Sie legten beide, jeder legte sich,
sie legten sich zusammen in den Löffel,
nur weil er hohl war, Schlaf vortäuschte,
—auch hohl war Vorwand und nur Widerspruch—
der Schlaf blieb kurz und kurz vorm Überkochen
hat beide, und ein jeder lag alleine,
derselbe Löffel abgeschöpft.

CHEFS AND SPOONS

And some will say: a chef's a chef.
All newly laundered, starched and spry
in snowfall or against a wall
that's whitewashed, chefs escape the eye
and then the spoons they hold are all
that stirs us, leaves us in no doubt:
the things we eat, the chefs dish out.

I don't think we should talk of soup
—the cabbage stock is neither here nor there—
for hunger is mere pretext for a beer,
and glut licks large and small spoons out of shape
and sits and counts the paces to the door.

The dolls outlive themselves,
the rooster dies before the chef
and crows elsewhere, and yet at times
the window panes will shiver in this town.
The dolls outlive themselves,
the rooster dies before the chef.

Flesh is the cause, a chef lives but in spirit.
Time passes, but the beef is still not done,
will last till later, till you sleep,
between your teeth will creep and lurk;
flesh is the cause, a chef lives but in spirit.

They both lay down, each one of them lay down,
together in the spoon they both lay down,
for it was hollow and it promised sleep—
yet hollow too was pretext and mere contradiction—
their sleep was short and shortly before boiling over
both, and now each one lay alone,
the self-same spoon skimmed off.

Hier ist kein Tod, der nicht zum Löffel führt,
und keine Liebe, die nicht ausgehöhlt
an Löffeln leidet und im Löffel bebt,
sich dreht, worum dreht, da sich alles
mit Löffeln nur um Löffel dreht.

Bleib Löffel, geh.
Wem Löffel, Löffel führt wohin.
Wann Löffel, Löffel kam zu spät.
Wer rührt mich, rührt mich und wohin.
Über und über wen balbiert.
Bleib, Löffel, geh—und sag mir nicht wohin.

So lernst du langsam Löffel unterscheiden,
kannst dich in Schubladen nicht mehr vermeiden,
du löffelst mit und läßt dich gern vertauschen,
du gibst dich blechern, gleichst dich an,
hörst deinen Nachbarn, wolltest gar nicht lauschen,
doch Löffel liegt dem Löffel an.

No death is here but leads back to the spoon,
and no love here but, hollowed out, at last
suffers from spoons and trembles in the spoon,
revolves, revolves round what, since everything
with spoons revolves round spoons and only spoons.

Then stay, spoon, go.
To whom spoon, spoon leads where.
What time spoon, spoon was late.
Who stirs me, stirs me where.
Over and over cuts whose hair.
Then stay, spoon, go—and do not tell me where.

So gradually you learn to tell the spoons apart,
no longer can avoid yourself in draws,
spoon with the rest and like to be mistaken,
act tinny and assimilate yourself,
can hear your neighbour, never meant to eavesdrop,
yet spoon fits into spoon, lies close to spoon.

SATURN

In diesem großen Haus
—von den Ratten,
die um den Abfluß wissen,
bis zu den Tauben,
die nichts wissen—
wohne ich und ahne vieles.

Kam spät nach Hause,
schloß mit dem Schlüssel
die Wohnung auf
und merkte beim Schlüsselsuchen,
daß ich einen Schlüssel brauche,
um bei mir einkehren zu können.

Hatte wohl Hunger,
aß noch ein Hühnchen
mit meinen Händen
und merkte beim Hühnchenessen,
daß ich ein kaltes und totes
Hühnchen aß.

Bückte mich dann,
zog beide Schuhe aus
und merkte beim Schuhausziehen,
daß wir uns bücken müssen,
wenn wir die Schuhe
ausziehen wollen.

Waagerecht lag ich,
rauchte die Zigarette
und war im Dunkeln gewiß,
daß jemand die Hand aufhielt,
als ich meiner Zigarette
die Asche abklopfte.

SATURN

In this big house—
from the rats
who know about the drains,
to the pigeons
who know nothing—
I live and suppose much.

Came home late,
opened the house
with my key
and noticed as I hunted for my key
that I needed a key
to enter my own home.

Was quite hungry,
ate a chicken
with my hands
and noticed as I ate the chicken
that I was eating a chicken
which was cold and dead.

Then stooped,
took off both shoes
and noticed as I took off my shoes
that we have to stoop
if we want to take
shoes off.

I lay horizontal,
smoked the cigarette,
and in the darkness was certain
that someone held out his open hand
when I knocked the ashes
from my cigarette.

Nachts kommt Saturn
und hält seine Hand auf.
Mit meiner Asche
putzt seine Zähne Saturn.
In seinen Rachen
werden wir steigen.

At night Saturn comes
and holds out his hand.
With my ashes, he
cleans his teeth, Saturn.
We shall climb
into his jaws.